Everyone at birth is given
a pair of ruby slippers.
There's no place like home –

But where is home?

THE WONDROUS
WIZDOM OF OZ

THE WONDROUS WIZDOM OF OZ

A Spiritual Odyssey

Christine Whitehead

Brandylane Publishers, Inc.
Richmond, Virginia

Copyright © 2004 by Christine Whitehead.
All rights reserved. No portion of this book may be reproduced in any form without the express permission of the publisher. Printed in the United States.

Library of Congress Control Number: 2003098757

Brandylane Publishers, Inc.
Richmond, Virginia
800-553-6922
www.brandylanepublishers.com

Cover concept and design by Jeanne Minnix

DEDICATION

This is dedicated to my munchkins—my sons, Justin, Kevin and Mark and granddaughter, Ashby. I am so happy to share this Earth adventure with all of you. It's in being together that we can better find our way.

To those I journey with—it has been an enlightening pleasure. To all my fellow travelers I have yet to meet—I can hardly wait to meet you.

To those in spirit who continue to guide me along the way—I so appreciate the messages that you send.

To the Universal Source—Mother/Father God—"Spirit," who provides for me and gives me strength to continue my journey—thank you for inviting me to "phone home."

I am blessed in all things.

CONTENTS

Chapter 1	Over the Rainbow	1
Chapter 2	Caught in the Fury	5
Chapter 3	A New Land	11
Chapter 4	The Wee People	14
Chapter 5	This Way or That?	22
Chapter 6	Is This the Garden of Eden?	26
Chapter 7	Lions and Tigers and Bears	34
Chapter 8	Detour	38
Chapter 9	Bell Out of Order—Please Knock	46
Chapter 10	United—One Can Stand	55
Chapter 11	Just a Walk in the Park?	60
Chapter 12	The Winged Monkeys	63
Chapter 13	Picking Themselves Up	67
Chapter 14	The Long Awaited Meeting	71
Chapter 15	To the Rescue	79
Chapter 16	Ashes, Ashes—We All Fall Down	84
Chapter 17	Seeking Validation	90
Chapter 18	You Have Always Had the Power	96
Chapter 19	Back to Her Original State	104

VISION

After watching the movie *The Wizard of Oz* for years, I was amazed to learn that the characters in this classic portray man quite well. Here on the planet Earth, we are all on a sacred journey to see the Wizard and to visit Oz. We all look for the magic—we're all looking for the way home.

My vision is to take you on a journey, a spiritual adventure—where finding oneself is the destination. This is a tour, guided by "Spirit," of my own individual interpretation of the wonderful 1939 MGM classical movie, *The Wizard of Oz*.

As a child, then later as a mother of three, I watched with delight in Dorothy's and Toto's adventure of being lost and trying to find their way home. Never did I see it other than as a movie for children.

It all started about 1992. I had a part-time practice of intuitive consulting with Tarot, astrology and teaching esoteric studies. One late afternoon, during a full day of consulting, it came to my attention that, at times, I would make reference to the characters in the movie such as, "You need to surrender Dorothy and let this issue go" or "You're just like the cowardly lion; your fears are overwhelming you!" I was puzzled as to why I had chosen these characters to make my point.

Later, while discussing some personal concerns of my own with a friend, her only comment was, "Well, Christine, we're not in Kansas anymore." I was struck by this response and was compelled to ask, "Why did you say that?" Her reply was unrevealing—"I really don't know."

But I knew it wasn't a simple answer; I felt there was something more profound involved; that my inner guidance was trying to tell me something, but what? In order to find out, I would have to take a concentrated look at this movie.

I immediately went to work. My gut feeling was telling me that if I were to watch—with devout attention through meditation—I would possibly be rewarded with the answers I sought. Eagerly, I found a quiet place, meditated and asked "Spirit" to help me. To my surprise and delight, I found many spiritual messages throughout! I was compelled to share these insights immediately with some of my friends and clients who all seemed to be enhanced by the different slant on this enchanting film. Many stated that they wanted to watch it again to see if they could draw their own messages beyond what I had shared with them.

A few years went by and, once again, I was making more but different references to the movie; it was time to take another look. I felt that "Spirit" was trying to encourage me to use this knowledge in some way, possibly in a workshop.

When I went looking for my old notes, I couldn't find them anywhere. I felt crushed because I had put so much time and energy into this project. I then realized that I would need to do this again. At first, I was like an angry child and said, "No, I'm not going to spend my time repeating this. If I can't find my notes, I'll just do something different." Suddenly, a warm energy surrounded me accompanied by an inner knowing that it wasn't a bad thing that I had lost my notes but instead a very good one. The inner voice of "Spirit" said that because of my spiritual immaturity early on, I had failed to pick up on everything; if I would review the scenes again, I would be treated to even more messages!

How could I resist? With child-like obedience, I watched the movie as I had before—in a meditative state. Once again, I listened to my inner voice and as promised, I was rewarded with much more insight! Even during the days that followed, I was given messages. I would hear my inner voice whisper, "Well, you were almost right" and then I would be given the correct information.

Once again, I could hardly wait to share this knowledge with others because I was moved by the comfort these simple but profound messages gave to me. I found myself wishing to share this but on a larger scale; instead of a creating a lecture series, it would become a book!

The *Wizard of Oz* has undergone many interpretations over time. I wish to share with you yet another one—an intuitive and spiritual look at this wonderful odyssey. It's my hope to inspire you to see the pictures beyond the pictures and the words between the words. In doing so, you may come to understand that your own life is a great drama worthy of a happy ending.

And so, our odyssey begins—

A MAP FOR YOUR JOURNEY

Throughout Dorothy's journey, you will find passages marked *WIZDOM* which are messages sent to me from "Spirit"—my inner voice—the voice of God along with my angels and master teachers in spirit. What you will read is direct dictation, unedited.

From the beginning of this venture, my inner spirit and angels have guided me. I have listened and followed their direction. Through prayer, meditation and a sincere desire to uncover sacred truths, I have been able to tap into this spiritual realm and openly receive messages. I wish to share these *WIZDOM* messages with you, the reader.

This inner voice resides in all of us; it is the voice of God. In addition, angels and spirit guides are sent daily by God to walk among us—to light the way and protect our steps.

Some people concern themselves with negative thoughts and beliefs regarding this type of transmission. Some think we are not worthy to talk directly to God and hear His voice; they suggest we need an intermediary, someone considered to have a better connection, so to speak. I suggest it is more negative and even dangerous to our spirit to ignore the voice within.

Over the years, I have been challenged by some for claiming to hear the voice of God. Disheartened, I would question myself on the validity of these messages. There are two things that have kept me believing that the voice I hear is God's; first, the messages I receive contain unconditional love and the other is the *Bible*.

In the *Bible*, you will read phrases such as "I heard a voice" or "an angel appeared to me." Visions, voices and angels are referred to throughout—

> *"For He shall give his angels charge over you,*
> *to keep you in all your ways.*
> *They shall bear you up in their hands, lest you*
> *dash your foot upon a stone."*
> —Psalm 91: 11-12

Personally, I do not believe that this type of transmission is unavailable at this time or any time; the voice of God is for all time.

SPECIAL GRATITUDE

Special gratitude to my sons who are a continuing source of inspiration for me—I have so enjoyed being your mother!

To my granddaughter, Ashby, who allows me to tap into my inner child and is always saying to me, "You're so funny, Grammy!"

To my mother, Rose Marie Corrieri Woody, and father, William L. Woody who gave me my foundation of faith and to my wonderful siblings; sisters, Pat and Jo Ann; my brothers, Michael and Paul who share my childhood memories.

To all my metaphysical teachers, especially, John Oliver. It was John who taught me how to be practical and stay grounded in my intuitive work; he made the learning fun.

To the Alchemist and Aquarian Bookshop in Richmond, Virginia, where I was allowed to evolve as an intuitive consultant and teacher. To all my clients and students—I learned so much from you.

To the Avalon Center in Richmond where I first introduced my manuscript for workshops; we shared several magnificent journeys down the yellow brick road!

To all my friends who have been and continue to be a great support to me in this endeavor; to the Circle of Light

& Love meditation group, especially Jackie McAllister—she gave of herself and her home where we grew spiritually and inspired one another.

To my friend, Bette Bowman, who tirelessly listens to all my life dramas; the good, the bad, and, oh yes, the sometimes ugly!

To the "Scarecrow", a powerful ally for many years; he taught me "how to fish."

To the Virginia IVF & Andrology Center's staff for their encouragement, especially Dennis Matt who gave me the time, space and computer to finish this project. An extra thanks to Amy Dotson, Leslie Gaskell, Daniel Graff and Kim Thayer who were there to correct my computer errors and would always say, "Let me show you an easier way to do that."

To Evelyn Hagen who discovered me and my manuscript on a rainy Sunday afternoon and, in true angelic fashion, guided me to Brandylane Publishers.

To my editor, Robert Pruett, who took a chance on me, a first-time author with an unusual manuscript. He inspired me to go within myself—deeper than I thought possible. What a journey that was!

Most of all, I offer this book up to God; showing that I have listened, written and spoken all the messages given to me. I am His humble servant with gratitude.

~ Be still and listen ~

*"Reality leaves a lot
to the imagination"*
—John Lennon

1

OVER THE RAINBOW

*"Some where over the rainbow
way up high,
there's a land that I heard of
once in a lullaby"*

Our scene opens: a young girl named Dorothy and her dog Toto are seen running away from someone. She feels threatened by one of her neighbors, a seemingly wretched woman, who is upset because Dorothy's dog has ruined her garden again. Dorothy runs home and tries desperately to tell her story about this harrowing event but the adults around her are too busy to listen. Dorothy's Auntie Em and Uncle Henry are preoccupied trying to save newborn chicks while the farm hands perform their many chores. Her Auntie Em tells her go somewhere and stay out of trouble. Dorothy poses a question to Toto, "Do you think there is such a place?"

WIZDOM

In your cellular memory, the soul's memory, there is a remembrance of a place just like this—a place you call home. A place you vaguely remember. In this place there is no struggle—no tears—only joy. You carry this memory with you throughout life.

You often view the Earth as a place of struggle and forget how it was meant to be. Look around at all of creation. See the beauty that lies before you and the power that is held within; the beautiful trees, birds, animals—the minerals of the Earth, flowers, mountain ranges, bodies of water, the air that cools and caresses, the sun and moon. Earth is a beautiful place, but somehow it has been forgotten.

Dare to dream of your world as being a peaceful one. Dare to dream that all mankind may enjoy the Earth as it was meant to be. Look at your world closely. Slow down and observe its majesty.

> "and the dreams that you dare to dream
> really do come true."

While Dorothy travels in her thoughts to a better place, Elvira Gulch, the outraged neighbor, arrives at Dorothy's home and insists upon taking Toto away for digging in her garden. She shows a document from the sheriff that reinforces this as Dorothy frantically defends Toto to no avail. Elvira Gulch leaves in a huff with the tiny dog under her arm and Dorothy is devastated.

Now, Toto is not about to be outdone by this petty tyrant so when the time is right, he jumps from the basket and makes his way back home.

Upon his return, Dorothy has a short-lived celebration, as she is aware that Elvira Gulch will only return. In her anxiety, she proceeds to act without much thought to consequences deciding to take Toto and run away.

WIZDOM

You have felt like running away. Man shares Dorothy's fear—fear of persecution—fear of losing—fear of separation—fear of not being in control.

A man who searches for control will never possess it—for Universal Law states: everything that is rightfully yours will come to you. Therefore, to try to possess another or another's possessions creates fear and it is this very fear that leads to a stronger desire to control.

Dorothy's dog was returned because he was rightfully

hers—remember this thought. You will find it useful on your journey.

Dorothy feels confused and frightened for she does not know about this "Universal Law." In her confusion, she takes leave of her home and all that is dear to her in order to protect her little dog from the clutches of the evil Elvira!

> *"If God be for us, who can be against us?"*
> —Romans 8:31

2

CAUGHT IN THE FURY

*"Do not let your hearts be troubled,
and do not let them be afraid"*
—Jesus, John 14:27

At the beginning of her journey, she runs into a man of magic—or shall we say, a man of illusion. His name is Professor Marvel—a reader of past, present and future. In talking with him, Dorothy learns that he is a world traveler so she suggests that maybe Toto and she could accompany him. Professor Marvel, sensing they are runaways and fearing for their safety, devises a plan to encourage them to return home.

He invites Dorothy into his wagon to consult his crystal ball regarding her plan. Unbeknownst to her, he reaches into the basket she carries and uses a photo for adlibbing his psychic ability. He only pretends to read from the crystal ball as he tells her that he can see a woman who is sick—that she is holding her heart because someone has broken it. Dorothy, convinced that he is speaking of her Auntie Em, frantically tells him that she will not be traveling with him after all and that she must return home as soon as possible. She has believed everything he has told her.

WIZDOM

People are put on your path to assist you in making right decisions. It is considered important to discern who is best to do this for you. It is not to be wasted upon those who cannot seem to get their own lives in order.

Now granted, Dorothy is a child who would believe most anything one told her, but there are many adults in the world today who do the same thing. They go from one friend to the next telling them of their plight in the hopes of finding the right answer. They may at times pay for the advice from psychics, astrologers, spiritual and religious advisors, psychotherapists, and others without spending much time checking the source of their counsel.

"KNOW THYSELF"
—Inscription on the Temple of Apollo at Delphi

Caught in the Fury

Dorothy leaves the man of magic in a great hurry; a storm is brewing. The environment around Dorothy suddenly matches her emotional turmoil. She senses that her Auntie Em needs her, but as she makes her way to the farm, she is pushed back by the accumulating winds.

Upon her arrival at the farmhouse, she calls out to her family in a panic but they have taken shelter and cannot hear her cries for help. The winds are picking up and a tornado is bearing down on the farm.

With Toto, she runs into the house for shelter. The forceful winds rip a piece of the house off, striking Dorothy on the head, knocking her unconscious.

> *"You don't need a weatherman*
> *to know which way the wind blows"*
> —Bob Dylan

WIZDOM

Do you sometimes feel the emotion of turmoil when you feel separated from God, your heavenly parent, the One you love most who created you in His likeness?

Have you been knocked unconscious by being caught up in your self and busy life that you have forgotten a greater power? Do you feel that life is something to be battled and not lived? Have you at times felt that your survival in the world has been left strictly in your hands? Questions to ponder.

Do not accept that you are separated from your Creator. Believe that He exists in everything around you such as the trees and flowers, the mountains and oceans, the sun and the moon.

Dorothy is now in the middle of the tornado. The house twirling and whirling about. She is amazed as she watches familiar people and things flying past her: men in a boat, cows and chickens, and Elvira Gulch dressed as a witch on her bicycle! Dorothy coveres her eyes in fear and the house begins to descend.

WIZDOM

Falling, falling, down, down—man's belief of "falling from grace"—a sinner who now walks the Earth in pain and disharmony, waiting only to return home.

This thought is only an illusion, dear one. A feeling of being rejected by the heavens when, clearly, it was your choice to travel to your new home—planet Earth.

Feel the beating of your heart and the fire within your

being. This is what you brought with you to this new but temporary home. You are here to create a new vision, a new world, your heaven here on Earth.

You are not separated from God. It is only an illusion. The Father and I are one – You can do this and more! – does this speak of separation? Who has told you these things that you believe? Look into your heart. FEEL the light and essence of your creator within you.

The house spirals down and comes to a hard landing; everything is still and the frightening event over. The house has settled—but where?

WIZDOM

Does this powerful tornado bring any memories to you—the emotion of being swept away and progressing through a tunnel, emerging abruptly into another dimension, vaguely making out faces, hearing undistinguished noises, feeling cold until wrapped, taking your first nourishment, bonding to those that are close to you or experiencing your new home and surroundings?

This is your birth. You have just traveled from one dimension to another and now inhabit a small and helpless body. What is to come in this new world?

3

A NEW LAND

*"Life imitates art far more
than art imitates life."*
—Oscar Wilde

Timidly, Dorothy approaches the door of the house. As she opens it, she is greatly surprised by her surroundings. It's a beautiful place! She is taken with the many colors of this new land but treads lightly for she does not know exactly where she is; she thinks she is over the rainbow!

*"I have a feeling we're not in Kansas
anymore—we must be over the rainbow."*
—Dorothy

As Dorothy surveys her new environment, an

immense ball of light glides towards her. Suddenly, a beautiful woman dressed like a queen emerges from this sphere carrying a magical wand and wearing a crown. We later learn that her name is Glinda.

Dorothy is surprised by her arrival then more surprised when Glinda inquires, "Are you a good witch or a bad witch?" Replying that she is neither one, Glinda then points to Toto and asks, "Well, is that a witch? Shocked, Dorothy emphatically tells her, "No!"

Glinda states that she is confused for she was told that a new witch had arrived and dropped a house on the Wicked Witch of the East. She then points to the crumpled body trapped under Dorothy's house with just the legs and feet showing.

Dorothy is amazed. She protests, declaring that the house does belong to her but she is not a witch; "Witches are old and ugly." Glinda tells Dorothy that this statement is not true and that she, herself, is a witch. This causes Dorothy more confusion than ever since she has never heard of a beautiful witch!

WIZDOM

One need not wonder why one witch can be ugly and another beautiful. It is not about "witches"—it is about personhood.

One may not be entirely beautiful to the eye, but

A New Land

if the deeds of that person are beautiful, the perception of physical beauty is changed. So it is with the beautiful person whose deeds are deceitful and ugly; the physical beauty will be changed in the eye of the beholder.

Giggles erupt from the bushes nearby. Dorothy looks around and questions the origin of the sounds that come from within the bed of flowers. At the same time, Glinda invites the "munchkins," the wee people of this new land, to come out of the bushes to meet Dorothy.

*"Come out, come, out wherever you are
and meet the young lady that fell from a star...*

SHE FELL FROM A STAR, SHE FELL VERY FAR"
—Glinda

WIZDOM

In the heavens, it is said, "It is from a star you came and it is to a star you shall return. Isn't it interesting that when one is famous, people refer to them as a "star?"

My loved one—everyone is a star and all you need is your remembrance of this.

4

THE WEE PEOPLE

*"When the first baby laughed for the first time,
its laugh broke into a thousand pieces
and they all went skipping about,
and that was the beginning of fairies."*
—J.M. Barrie

Who are these small people called "munchkins?" Could they represent what we fondly refer to as the "wee people" or fairies? They do exist among the flowers and are the living energy of the lovely place that Dorothy has landed.

WIZDOM

Ah, the fairies of your land live among the trees, within the center of flowers and each blade of grass in order

The Wee People

that they not be lonely, for they are a chummy lot! This is where they enjoy being—nurturing the trees and the flowers, the quiet ones, the non-speakers—the ones who unselfishly give of themselves to the service of the Earth.

Go, dear one, and join them in the garden and the forest. There you will experience a different world. Forget the chaos that whirls around you. Find the peace and harmony that resides within the boundaries of nature and embraces the world. Should you invite them into your life, they may come, but BEWARE—a lot of humor and play travels with them.

Do you dare to be happy? Do you dare to laugh? Do you dare to drop the seriousness of your life to play? Do you dare? Look around and you might catch a glimpse of them—they are waiting.

The munchkins are thrilled to meet Dorothy. The wicked witch's death creates a time for celebration and praise. Once again, Dorothy tries to explain the events of the tornado to everyone because she truly did not deliberately kill the witch. Nonetheless, a great celebration commences.

"DING DONG, THE WITCH IS DEAD!"

WIZDOM

Anytime evil is squelched, there is cause for celebration. All life begins in the purest of form. When bacteria occurs in the body and attacks human cells, there is a need to combat it. When a fire occurs in the forest, there is a need to stamp it out. When evil in any form surrounds a person or place, there is a desire to destroy it before it invades and completely takes over.

Evil can arrive in many forms; you must be ever vigilant. Evil takes its silent path through despair, loneliness and hopelessness. You need to be on the lookout for thoughts that cause you great despair and create within you a sense of hopelessness. These thoughts are dangerous invaders of the soul.

You must take care of yourself during these times. Eat well, take walks in nature, get the right amount of sleep, and, most importantly, use the power of prayer. The evil that tries to penetrate your spirit will feel pushed out and away and will be unable to find a dwelling place within you.

In the midst of their celebrating, another witch appears from a cloud of smoke. Her sudden appearance abruptly stops the celebration, for she is also wicked and feared.

The Wee People

"And who knows which is which and who is who,
up and down, and in the end,
it's only round and round and round."
—Pink Floyd

Dorothy looks to Glinda questioning, "I thought you said she was dead." Glinda responds by saying that the witch killed was the Wicked Witch of the East and the one that has just arrived is her sister, the Wicked Witch of the West.

The darkened figure of a woman screeches, "Who killed my sister?" Then, looking at Dorothy hard, she asks, "Was it you?" Frightened, Dorothy tries to defend herself as she explains the terrible tornado and how everything that occurred was out of her control.

Glinda interrupts their encounter by asking the wicked witch if she has forgotten her sister's ruby red slippers, which abruptly diverts her attention away from Dorothy. The witch looks to her sister's feet jutting out from under the house and sees the slippers just in time to watch them disappear—"What have you done with them?"

Dorothy is greatly surprised, for the slippers, the beautiful ruby red slippers of the Wicked Witch of the

East, are now on her feet! The dark Witch of the West is horrified at this sudden transference and demands them back! Glinda cautions Dorothy. "Keep tight inside of them. Their magic must be very powerful!"

WIZDOM

Have you not, at times, looked at another and felt the desire to possess what he or she has obtained through personal inheritance or endeavors?

We ask you to look to your personal talents and cultivate them as one tends an abundant garden. You have been given everything you need for your journey; the lesson here is to acknowledge this. Be grateful for what you have been given and through cultivation you will achieve.

By showing gratitude for what your Creator has already bestowed, you create a space of manifesting your Earth reality as a co-creator with Him; beginning with gratitude and continuing with faith.

The wicked witch threatens Glinda and tells her to stay out of her unfinished business with Dorothy. Unafraid of her taunting, Glinda tells her to leave before someone drops a house on her.

The Wee People

Forced to go, the wicked witch vows revenge proclaiming to Dorothy, "I'll get you my pretty—and your little dog, too!" She departs as dramatically as she arrived—in a cloud of threats and smoke.

It is now quite clear that Dorothy needs to leave this beautiful place. She wants to go back home but realizes that she can't go back the way she came.

She doesn't know how to begin.

"It sounded as if the streets were running,
And then the streets stood still.
Eclipse was all we could see at the window,
And awe was all we could feel"
—Emily Dickinson

Glinda suggests that she seek the wisdom of the wonderful Wizard of Oz who lives in the Emerald City. Dorothy asks, "How do I get there"? Glinda tells her to follow the yellow brick road that lies before her. Sensing Dorothy's apprehension as to how or where to begin, Glinda tells her, "It is always best to start at the beginning."

Unknowingly, as Dorothy takes her first step on the yellow brick road, she also takes her first step on the path of illumination; her soul's path. There will be no turning back!

> *"The road to the City of Emeralds
> is paved with yellow brick."*
> — L. Frank Baum

WIZDOM

So many times you have looked back at your life to evaluate where you have been while trying to see what lies ahead. In looking in these very different directions, you may stumble and fall. You are to look only to the next step ahead while asking for guidance and protection from above. You are not to worry about the following step; that is where you shall apply your faith, knowing that each step will lead you to the next.

Your journey to this planet Earth begins with your first breath and ends with your last. Everything in between is like "cream" in the middle of a cookie—to be savored and enjoyed. Life has the possibility to be as whimsical as fairy tales. Enjoy all things, including what you perceive as good and what you perceive as bad, for all of this is your creation. It is your life!

There will be times when you are the victim and at times the victor. All are moments to be enjoyed. The prize in all of this is the ability to learn from the lessons presented to you and to transcend your perceptions through non-judgement, and just be.

The Wee People

"Let It Be"
—Paul McCartney

With a resounding send off, the munchkins say goodbye to Dorothy—"Goodbye, goodbye" as she skips down the yellow brick road, turning at times to wave farewell to the wee people of Munchkinland.

"—because, because, because, because, because! Because of the wonderful things he does"

5

THIS WAY OR THAT?

*"I am always under direct inspiration;
I make right decisions, quickly."*
—Florence Shinn

Finding herself at a fork in the road, Dorothy is puzzled and cannot decide which direction to take. There are many paths to a destination. She will recognize decision making as one of her many human gifts—free choice.

WIZDOM

Now, with free choice, comes the dreaded word—"responsibility." You all want freedom and to make your own choices, but are you willing to take the responsibility of making a mistake—falling on your face in front of

This Way or That?

everyone—be shown imperfect? Egad!

So, you ask your family, friends and work associates what to do? In the end, you might make the choice you wanted to in the first place, but now you have someone to blame if you fail.

You may decide to cancel your own thinking and go a different way because you trust someone else's thinking better than your own. Once again, you may not see this act as a mistake and you will think you have a right to complain and blame others if things don't work out right.

The possibility of failing creates fear and it is this very fear that will keep you from making right choices for yourself. Consequently, you will take limited risks in life. This fear may cause you to wonder for many years, "What could have been?"

Think back. When you were young and playing with your friends, did you want them to make your choices for you? When you saw a bike you liked, did you wait and ask a friend "if" you should ride that bike or another? No, you didn't. You tried to be "first," you called "first" and if you didn't get it, you raged, "I was first!"

Where have you put that child?

Now granted, you can't all be first, but you all deserve first. You should never give away your power to make choices. Letting someone decide for you is allowing someone else to live your life.

You must trust yourself and the ability within you to

make right choices.

Dorothy meets a scarecrow hanging from a post in a field; he is soon to become her friend and fellow traveler. He represents yet another one of her gifts—logic. Dorothy will be taught how to make the necessary choices ahead and find "logic" a powerful ally on her journey.

Upon their meeting, the scarecrow says that he feels like a failure because he doesn't have a brain and isn't even good at scaring crows. Great detail is expressed about what he would do if he "only had a brain." Dorothy tells him of her plight and how she plans to visit the Wizard of Oz for his help. The scarecrow wonders aloud if this mysterious wizard could possibly grant his wish for a brain. Believing in the wizard's abilities, Dorothy invites him to travel with her to Emerald City. As they link up, arm in arm, a decision is made as to which direction to take.

WIZDOM

In linking up with the conscious mind and trusting your ability to make right decisions, you tap into a powerful source. You will rely on this connection to make the many choices that are offered in your life; the mind takes in information and transforms it to understanding.

This is man's ability to THINK—a wonderful gift to be given. Don't be so eager to give it away.

6

IS THIS THE GARDEN OF EDEN?

"Love is fruit in season at all times, and within reach of every hand."
—Mother Theresa

Taking a break from their mission, Dorothy is hungry and spies several trees with ripened apples. As she reaches to pick one from a branch, the outraged living tree smacks her hand. Dorothy is appalled at this reprimand!

WIZDOM

Who is at fault here? Dorothy, by her grabbing, or the tree for smacking her hand? Clearly, Dorothy is for she has shown little respect for the tree—unconsciously reaching for the apples without permission.

Is This the Garden of Eden?

Dorothy had no knowing, no memory, that the tree, even though it appeared as an inanimate object, was the living energetic property of the Earth. Dorothy's lesson—and yours—is respect for the natural world.

Mankind needs to come to a fuller understanding, as some already have, that trees and boulders are not meaningless objects that need to be removed for another parking lot or building. Careful consideration must be given before their removal.

There is a great need to acquire a healthy respect for Mother Earth; a need to acknowledge that polluting and destroying for profit, without giving much thought to what this means to the further existence of the Earth and its inhabitants, threatens everyone. There is a great need to slow down the destruction. You must take a moment to think about what its bounty and beauty brings to you.

How sad that fish must swim in polluted water; that flowers grow in toxic soil; how sad that birds fly through the fog of new technologies; and how very sad for the humans of the Earth to play a part in this quiet but definite destruction.

Man worries about war and annihilation while the very things that give him life are slowly and silently being destroyed. You must regard these thoughts—make a promise to yourself that each day you will honor the Earth in some way; giving gratitude for the bounty that lies before you and pass your love and respect for the Earth to the children who will follow.

In trying to help Dorothy, the scarecrow tricks the trees into releasing their apples. He taunts them by insulting the ripeness of their fruit—"She doesn't like little green worms." The trees react by tossing their apples like weapons at him, leaving plenty at her feet for rightful taking!

The trees have thrown apples everywhere! While looking for stray ones in the grass, Dorothy comes upon a tin foot attached to a tin man. He tries to speak but he can't; he has become rusted by standing in the forest.

Unable to open his mouth, he can only mumble, "Oil can." At first, they can barely understand him but when they realize what he is saying, they find the can of oil nearby and apply it to the edges of his mouth. Fully greased, he says, "My elbow—my arm." Finding much relief in moving his arm that had been fixed in the air, holding an axe, he says, "I've held that axe up for ages!"

WIZDOM

What axe have you been holding up. What axe have you had to grind, as they say?

The inability to let go of grudges can bring about strong emotions within you causing stiffness in the physical

Is This the Garden of Eden?

body. This can interfere not only with your emotional ability to move forward in your life but can also affect physical movement.

By living in the past you are relieved of the responsibility of being in the present moment—the place where the creation of future moments is manifested.

Manifesting, creating with your Creator, cannot be accomplished while living in the past. Say, for example, that you had some dough in front of you to make bread for today—but instead of using the fresh dough, you used the dough from last week or last month. You will not be able to create a fresh loaf of delicious bread from yesterday's dough. This is a parable—you cannot create a bright new today while standing in the heartache of yesterday.

Lay your axe down, and greet your day with revelry.

After oiling the tin man, Dorothy exclaims, "Now, you're perfect!" But tin man laments that he is far from perfect; he feels hollow inside because the tinsmith failed to give him a heart.

Dorothy and the scarecrow whisper to each other; the tin man is invited to be a part of their journey to seek the help of the wizard. Believing the search for a heart is for the tin man, Dorothy is about to learn another lesson;

it is her search as well!

WIZDOM

You have now come to a pivotal point in your existence—the place where you can truly feel, not just experience life.

You have come into existence to learn but more importantly you have come to "feel" the expression of love and its divine healing force. This "emotion" is quite strange. It can turn a human being inside out; it can bring much joy and at times great sorrow.

You ask yourself, "Why should I feel if there is a chance for sorrow?" We say that this extraordinary emotion is most important. It is the act of feeling that lets you know that you are truly alive!

As they continue their quest, the wicked witch appears on the roof of a house in the woods. Very unhappy with Dorothy's companions, she declares that bad things will happen to both of them if they decide to help her; she threatens to make a bee hive out of the tin man and stuff a mattress with the scarecrow! To confirm her power, she throws a conjured ball of fire on the scarecrow.

He starts screaming, "I'm burning, I'm burning!" Her horrible action ignites the scarecrow not just physically but emotionally as well. As the flame is extinguished, he vows to escort Dorothy to the Emerald City safely whether he receives a brain or not! The tin man chimes in. He too will remain at Dorothy's side whether he receives a heart or not. They present to the witch a strong, impassioned united front!

Dorothy is moved by their proclamations; "You're the best friends anybody ever had and, it's funny, but I feel as if I've known you all the time, but I couldn't have, could I? Still, I wish I could remember."

*"Greater love hath no man than this,
that a man lay down his life for his friends."*
—John 15:13

WIZDOM

You have all seen others you feel you have known before. You question where it might have been only to realize that you have never met. We say, it is the light within them and the energy without that you recognize. It is like a person who can be distinguished by the cologne they wear.

Souls who have traveled together before have an instant recognition of one another and become a source of support and inspiration. They may take on different roles per lifetime supporting their soul's growth through many lessons.

Not all meetings will be pleasant ones. At times, your spiritual growth will come through lessons of strife creating a need within you to gain further understanding, forgiveness and unconditional love.

You must look to the ones who support your mission and purpose in life and bless them all—both the perceived good and bad, for they inspire the whole journey.

You see, it is very easy to bless all the good things and people in your life. It is far more challenging to bless the not so good as well; but you are asked to try. Time will be your teacher; what seems bad in the present moment will later show itself to be a small stepping stone to something more fortunate.

You are actors in this movie, "life." How would you learn to forgive if you had no one to forgive? How would you enjoy the victories without the battles? This journey of yours is an exciting one; we watch from afar; we feel your pain as well as your elation; they are seen as one and the same. For you see, it is all these emotions that make up your life!

Is This the Garden of Eden?

"All the world's a stage, and all the men and women merely players. They have their exits and their entrances, and one man in his time plays many parts."
—William Shakespeare

7

LIONS AND TIGERS AND BEARS

"Yea, though I walk through the valley of the shadow of death, I will fear no evil."
—23rd Psalm

As they make their way through the darkness, fear takes over. The scarecrow says, "I think it will get darker before it gets lighter"—the proverbial darkness before the dawn.

Dorothy questions if they will meet any wild animals on their way. The tin man says they might—like "lions and tigers and bears!" Just as these words are spoken, they are faced with their fear; a lion jumps into their path frightening and intimidating them—he wants to fight. It's only when Toto is threatened that Dorothy is able to muster up some courage to stop this obnoxious cat with a slap on the face!

WIZDOM

When you are afraid, your fears take on a life of their own. You must face them down. You must have faith to move forward and not be paralyzed by the sordid imaginings of your mind.

"Faith" is just another word in your vocabulary until you demonstrate a need to possess it. At first you might feel that you cannot find it—that it is something others have but you do not. But it is upon failing and falling again and again—feeling that all is lost, that faith can be found.

When all seems to be falling apart, grow quiet and listen to the voice within to affirm that, no matter what takes place, you are fine. No matter what is thrown at you, it can be managed. No matter the outcome, it is the Divine Plan. Then you can move forward with no regrets, no recriminations. In mastering this lesson, you become "faithful," and fear will leave you.

Congratulations! You now have an extremely important ingredient to move you forward on this adventure of Self—the gift of courage gained through faith. When in doubt, affirm –

Everything is fine (breathe)
Everything is fine (breathe)
Everything is fine (breathe)
Everything in Divine Time (breathe)

The lion cries excessively over Dorothy's punishment. Through his tears and sobs, he tells them that he acts mean because he is really afraid and actually has no courage at all!

WIZDOM

Lions and tigers and humans—you are the same. A person will intimidate and lash out at others when he feels threatened and lacks self worth; they who roar the loudest feel the smallest. Feeling torn down, they wish to bring others down—and so it goes.

When someone lashes out, it may come at a time when that person needs love the most. On the opposite hand, you, the recipient, will be given an extraordinary opportunity to develop patience, compassion, forgiveness and unconditional love. Should you acknowledge this as an opportunity, you will have broken the chain; you become the victor and not the victim.

Dorothy, the tin man, and scarecrow invite the lion

to share in their quest; he could ask for the gift of courage. Together, they are about to learn their finest lessons!

"If only I had a brain,"
"a heart,"
"the nerve,"
"a home"

WIZDOM

"If only, if only. . ." Is this how you wish to go through this life? "If only I had earned more money"—If only I had been married"—"If only I had stayed single"—"If only I had furthered my education"; an endless list to ponder.

You must make the very best of what life has given you, and in doing so, you may find talents and gifts yet to tap. Everyone, and we repeat, everyone has all the necessary gifts to carry him or her through their life lessons. What loving parent would put their child in a foreign land without all his necessities?

Look within. Be grateful for what has been given and know that your Almighty Father has taken care of your needs before the asking. Be courageous in all endeavors and never feel slighted, for your Father does not have favorites.

8

DETOUR

*"Poppies,
Poppies will put them to sleep."*
—The Witch

In the meantime, the wicked witch spies on them in her crystal ball as she thinks of a potion to block their way to the city. She says, "Something with poison in it—something attractive to the eye and soothing to the smell."

A trap is created in a field of poppies!

WIZDOM

You must be very careful of what entices you and leads you off course, for that may be the very thing that will put your spirit into a deep sleep. Be aware of anyone or anything that exhibits power over you—a power that, in time, wears away confidence, creates guilt and causes inner recriminations.

Look at possible addictions—the crutches you might have chosen.

CIGARETTES
ALCOHOL
DRUGS
SEXUAL ADDICTION
FOOD
WORK

S-L-E-E-P, S-L-E-E-P. What do you feel when you see these words? Hear the message, feel the power of this hypnotic suggestion—S-L-E-E-P.

You all can become weary of your "Earth walk." When you feel this way, there is of course, a need to rejuvenate the self—"rejuvenation" being the key word; not "numbing."

Taking time out to rejuvenate the body is a good practice. Walking, praying, meditating are ways of rejuvenation—a refreshing way to enliven the spirit in order to move forward.

Enticements of escape, however, slow you down and create guilt—"I'll quit tomorrow." You lose your initial focus of "looking for the way home." You fall asleep and become deadened to life.

We give you a guide for "intentional" living assisting the mindfulness of your journey.

FORMULA
A Guide for Intentional Living

Element	Materialized >	Physical >	Spiritual
Water	Water	Cleansing	Purity
Air	Oxygen	Breath	Lightness of Being
Earth	Nature	Food	Grounding
Fire	Passion	Meditation	Love

It is a blending of heaven and earth.

WATER: Cleansing/Purity

It is important that the body get plenty of good drinking water everyday; don't allow it to dehydrate. Also, it would benefit the body to shower with the intent of cleansing the energy field that surrounds it. As you go through your day, not only does your body become unclean, the energetic field surrounding you will collect negative debris from the fields of others. Water is used in many blessing ceremonies to rid an area or a person of negative energy and is a life-giving source.

Detour

OXYGEN: *Breath/Lightness of Being*

Take time to breathe. Exercise. Inhale deeply with the intent to oxygenate your body. Feel each breath as it runs through you. Exhale with the intent of allowing the toxic breath out. The physical body will enjoy the newness of air and the soul will enjoy the feeling of lightness and calm; being one with each breath. This is a life-giving source.

NATURE: *Food/Grounding*

The body, mind, and spirit of man are brought into a state of peace in the midst of nature. Man needs to walk the Earth with intent, for it is his temporary home. People can, without knowing, become detached from their environment by the act of staying busy. They eventually find themselves surrounded by much noise and aggravation. The food of the Earth provides man with his physical need for nourishment while his spirit is imbued by the solitude it finds in nature. This is a life-giving source.

MEDITATION: *Passion/Love*

People look to each other for passion and fire but it is important for each individual to find this within himself first. Think of a comet that comes from the heavens in a burst of flames; this energy lies within every soul creating a burning desire and intent to come forth and create. It enhances the physical body to enjoy physical passion and it strengthens the soul to understand unconditional love. Through the art of meditation both passion and love can be found. Meditation brings the physical and spiritual aspects of man into a higher dimension and vibration in an unconditional manner; this IS the Life Source.

Live your life, dear ones, with awareness, intention and Oneness.

As our unaware travelers exit the woods, they see the splendor of Emerald City! With great delight, they run through the poppy field to get there. In the midst of the excitement, Dorothy suddenly feels tired and informs the others that she needs to lie down. The scarecrow panics saying, "You can't—we're nearly there!" Dorothy says that she can't go any farther and must rest for only a minute. She then lies down and falls into a deep sleep.

WIZDOM

Be strong. You will grow weary at times, but remember, you could be very close to your goal!

As they discuss how to help Dorothy to her feet, Toto and the lion lapse into a deep sleep. Sensing this as a spell formulated by wicked witch, the tin man and scarecrow start yelling for help.

The witch watches their hysterics unfold through her crystal ball proclaiming, "It's no use screaming; no one will hear you." They continue to call out for help when, without a cloud in the sky, snow begins to fall upon the poppies.

But the scarecrow does not fall under the witch's spell because of his "logic" and strong will. His calling out symbolizes his inner knowing that his environment is out of control and the need to call for higher assistance.

WIZDOM

There is knowledge within the soul that recognizes the need for assistance. It is profound wisdom that will allow you to ask for help. So many times, man is reluctant to humble himself and admit he cannot control his immediate environment or circumstances.

Let it be known; it is through the state of being humble and asking for help that deliverance from one's addictions and endangerment can be overcome and prayers are best answered.

Waving her magic wand, Glinda comes to their rescue by creating snow. She awakens them not just from their physical sleep but their spiritual one as well—the white snow representing purity and renewal. Glinda is Dorothy's protector—a celestial being who has answered their cry for help.

The snow floats quietly down as everyone slowly awakens. Relieved, the scarecrow and lion exclaim, "Dorothy, you're waking up!"

As they come to their feet, they realize that the tin man will need a little extra help from his friends for he has once again rusted from the snow and cannot move.

With much care, they mobilize him. Now, everyone is ready!

The evil witch becomes frustrated with this sudden turn of events—"Curses, curses, somebody always helps that girl!" She vows not to give up!

> *"Everyone of us gets through the tough times because someone is there, standing in the gap to close it for us."*
> —Oprah Winfrey

WIZDOM

Help is only a call away. You are together with your loved ones and strangers on this miraculous journey called

Detour

life. You cannot do another's personal journey but you can assist one another.

There will be times when assistance will come from another being on your planet; know that it is heaven that sends them to you.

We also guide you to help others; know that you can earn your wings here on the planet by helping another to fly.

You must let it be known to the powers that be that you are a child of the Creator—sheep from His flock. Let no wrong doing come to you as you proclaim this to the world!

Beckoning them with its massive beauty, Emerald City stands off in the distance. All previous events are suddenly forgotten as they run forward to meet their future!

Hold on to your breath, hold on to your heart,
hold on to your hope ~~
March up to the gate and bid it open, open
—The Wonderful Wizard of Oz

9

BELL OUT OF ORDER— PLEASE KNOCK

*"Ask and it shall be given you,
seek, and ye shall find,
knock and the door will open unto you"*
—Mathew 7:7

As they rush towards the door, they ring a large attached bell. A man immediately appears and asks, "Can't you read?"

He points to a sign—

**Bell out of order—
Please knock**

Dorothy and friends are on the threshold of entering the wizard's castle. This moment is symbolic of

Dorothy's inner journey; upon knocking on the door, she knocks on the door of her own heart, the very place she will find the wizard.

WIZDOM

**Open, open—allow your heart to open. You say it has been wounded, but we say, as long as your heart remains shut, it cannot be filled.

> *"More room in an open heart"*
> —Carly Simon

Once again, they are greeted by the irritable doorman; "What do you want?" They answer, "We want to see the wizard"

"The wizard? But nobody can see the Great Oz. Nobody's ever seen the Great Oz! Even I've never seen him." Dorothy is puzzled—"So how do you know there is one?"

WIZDOM

A very good question from someone so small. How do

you know that the one you call God truly exists. Is it because you have been told and you believe? And, who taught you how to believe?

You can be taught many things but not " how to believe." You either believe or not—the state of believing something comes from within each of you. It has to "fit," you might say.

You can teach yourself to believe by looking around you. Countless and magnificent things in nature not only surround you on Earth but in your solar system as well. In nature, you will find balance.

All is perfect, and perfection IS God.

Dorothy's friends protest. They point to the ruby slippers on Dorothy's small feet as their right to see the wizard. The doorman, gazing upon the sparkling slippers, allows their entry.

WIZDOM

The shoes represent Dorothy's inheritance—the color red symbolizing her desire and sovereign right to enter.

Enter as a little child with wide, unabashed intent. Ask with the innocence of a child who knows his or her needs and expects them to be met.

Each one of you wears the ruby red slippers—it is called your "inheritance." The acceptance of this will take you into God's Kingdom.

It is by desire you arrive; it is through intent that you enter.

There is much celebration when Dorothy and her companions enter. They ride in a carriage drawn by a "horse of a different color!" She is unaware that the actual changing of the horse's color represents the ever-changing energy that encompasses her own energetic field. The colors they speak of are not just a figure of speech in the land of OZ. The people there can see the auras of horses as well as other things. Dorothy will come to understand that nothing is as it appears in this curious city!

Remembering her mission, she asks if this horse-drawn cab will take her to the wizard. The reply is resounding "yes" but first they will be taken to a place to tidy up. They are all in agreement; their journey has been long and they don't want to meet with the wizard in such disarray.

The tin man is shined, the scarecrow is stuffed, the lion curled and manicured and Dorothy primped. Now, they are ready.

WIZDOM

Prior to going before the one he calls God, humans wish to be cleansed of all transgressions; made pure. Know, dear one, that you are already perfect in His eyes, for you are His creation!

It saddens those already in the dimension of God's Kingdom that you have yet to learn this. You have allowed others to tell you of your perfection and imperfection. This creates within you a persona that may not be you in the truest sense.

If you were to be left alone among nature and recognized its perfection, you would have an inner knowing of your own.

Shut out the murmurs of those who wish to tell you how imperfect you are. Stand in nature and know that you are a genuine part of this beautiful creation called Earth.

After this joyful preparation, the attention of everyone in the city suddenly shifts; the wicked witch appears in the sky writing a message with smoke trails from her broom:

Bell Out of Order—Please Knock

"SURRENDER DOROTHY"

The people of the city scurry about crying, "Who is Dorothy—who is Dorothy?" Dorothy and friends feel the need to see the wizard as soon as possible! There is chaos in the city.

WIZDOM

The word surrender sometimes makes people think of losing. As you continue to look at life in a broader manner, surrender means quit fighting yourself—quit fighting others—lay down your arms. Don't fight the tides of your emotions. Let your tears fall down upon the Earth; relax and let go of the torment inside of you.

Surrender to the will of heaven. All of it is a beautiful plan—accepting that the will of God prevails; accepting that you may not understand the "whys" and the "how comes," yet trusting just the same.

Heaven is being at peace with your God, self and others. Know that you cannot find inner tranquility as long as there is an ounce of fight within.

Surrender so that you can begin to create your Heaven on Earth.

"Thy Will Be Done; On Earth as it is in Heaven."
—Mathew 6:10

Now, in the outer drama, the wicked witch wants Dorothy to surrender to her. But, as this story unfolds, it becomes clear that an inner drama of greater proportion is taking place. Manifested in form as the wicked witch, the dark side of Dorothy calls for her attention.

It is now time for Dorothy to confront her shadow—her guilt and shame—the place where she brings judgment upon herself. Everyone in the palace is fearful for they have a hidden understanding of this difficult task.

WIZDOM

You will need to explore the self and create a space of acceptance for who you are this lifetime. This will require looking into the aspects of the self that bring about dissatisfaction, feelings of guilt and inner recriminations; the nagging, haunting inner dialogue you would rather ignore.

Humans have an innate ability, at times, to simply deny their own perceived unlikable traits, yet may project these imperfect images upon others. This enables them to point a finger at another and judge.

If you do feel judgmental regarding another being, you might look within and ask, "What is it about myself, similar to this person, that I so dislike?" Measure then whether it truly warrants change and go about the business of transforming yourself. You will make more progress by changing yourself than another.

You were born into this world perfect. It is only through man's eyes that imperfection is seen.

Everyone in the city is terrified by the witch's presence but the doorman tries to calm them by saying everything is fine and suggesting they all go home. Once again, Dorothy and her friends beg to see the wizard but are told to wait. They are nervous during this trial but try not to let their apprehension overwhelm them. They all need courage!

"What makes a king out of a slave?
COURAGE"
—The Cowardly Lion

WIZDOM

Courage is another word for faith. When you have faith you automatically have courage.

Believe that everything you experience on a daily basis gives you an opportunity to experience the Earth in a loving manner—challenges at every point—an opportunity every day with a belief that all things unfold in a perfect manner in perfect timing. In the practice of this, you will develop a deeper faith bringing forth the courage you so desire.

10

UNITED—ONE CAN STAND

"All for one and one for all"
—A. Dumas

They are now told to go away; they cannot see the wizard. Devastated, Dorothy starts to cry; her last hope is dashed. She feels lost forever, never to return home. The doorman dissolves into tears as he listens to Dorothy's heartache and relents; they are told they will be allowed to see the wizard after all. The door opens for them!

Going down the hallway, they exhibit fear of this unknown venture; they shake and tremble from fright. They decide to link arms to support one another. At this crucial point, it is valuable to know that the characters in Dorothy's drama are no longer separate. As they link arms, you will notice that even though they remain different to the eye, they are really one unit belonging to Dorothy:

The scarecrow; her logic
The tin man; her emotional self
The endearing lion; her fear

Now, looking closer still, can you see yourself in Dorothy—the child of innocence, seeker of the wizard—trying to get home? You and Dorothy are one and seek the same! We can now move forward knowing our characters are not separate but one. They exhibit this as they march down the hallway with arms linked— symbolic of the connection of the body, mind and spirit of man.

Terrified, they push themselves forward. Upon reaching the end of the hallway they are startled by a frightening face near the ceiling of the inner temple accompanied by a terrible thundering in the air; they all shake with fear.

"Come forward—who are you?"

Each one of them is called forward to identify himself to the wizard and tell him why they have come; they tremble with thoughts of impending doom!

WIZDOM

In the past, some of you have cowered before the one you call God while asking for His intercession in your life; you may not feel justified in the asking.

If you could sense your God as a loving parent, not apart from yourself, you would endure less apprehension; you would hold a confidence within your being that all your prayers are answered before the beseeching.

Sensing their fear, the wizard hurls insults at them! Dorothy is indignant! She stands up for herself and the others but is immediately silenced. Abruptly, the wizard surprises them by agreeing to grant all their wishes.

The excitement they experience is short-lived as they learn his gifts are conditional; he demands the broom of the wicked witch to prove themselves worthy!

WIZDOM

You may at times wish to endear yourself to God through good works for others. While this is a good endeavor, you must understand that your mere presence upon the Earth makes you quite dear.

In the eyes of God, you are most worthy. Your possible misunderstanding of this truth can hinder the way you perceive goodness in your life and whether you deserve to be happy.

All your needs are known by your Heavenly Father and are given to you; you are meant to be victorious in your Earth venture. You are meant to experience the joy that is available to you.

Joy comes from a sense of well-being—a connection to heaven and Earth. If feelings of separation and unworthiness prevail, it is not a wizard outside of yourself who can give this to you. It can only be gained from a total connection to the God that lives within you.

Fearful of the wizard's demand, they quibble with him but he shouts at them, "Go!" They try to reason with him but he only shouts louder, "GO!" They can't leave fast enough; the lion makes his exit, diving through the nearest window.

WIZDOM

Fear is an illusion that resides in your mind and heart. Every time you demolish a fear, there is a rebuilding of the self. Real freedom takes place when you face down your fears, one by one, and are no longer bound by them.

You must not try to avoid them—go around them—or hide from them. You may be avoiding the very challenge that may set you free. Every time you face your fears head on, you gain strength and grow.

"DEAL WITH IT"
—Tom Hanks

11

JUST A WALK IN THE PARK?

"You're on the road but you've got no destination—you're in the mud, in the maze of her imagination."
—Bono (of U2)

Looking for the witch's castle, Dorothy and her friends walk dubiously in a forest that appears haunted; they see a sign of warning—

"I'D TURN BACK IF I WERE YOU."

The scarecrow says, "I think there are spooks in here." The tin man replies, "That's ridiculous"—when, suddenly, an unknown force picks him up and slams him to the ground!

Now, once again, fear is the true culprit that affects their desire to go any farther. They all become terrified as the lion starts his chant, "I do believe in spooks, I do, I do, I do!" that not only affirms his fear but also instills fear in those around him. They become paralyzed by their mind's imaging and are unaware of the attack to come.

WIZDOM

Affirm your life to the positive. For every negative thought, replace it with a positive one. It is through the power of thought that all your tomorrows are created; you are to be ever vigilant of how they are to be used.

You must choose your words carefully. They can be your undoing. Don't give in to your fears and allow them to take over. Watch your words and the words of others. Ponder this: all that you think and all that you say—IS!

There will be times when others will suggest you turn back should you discover a different path to walk. You will get messages and signs from others wishing to corrupt your desire to seek your own answers. There will be people calling you a heretic for searching beyond posted beliefs.

It scares them that you might uncover truths that will shake some roots of religious doctrine. Will you allow their means of coercion? Remember you have free choice and a will to use it. You are not bound by others' truths. You are meant to question and explore.

You were told to have only one God before you. You were not told to have only one religion—only one belief—or just one path to follow.

If you are to make a transformation in your life, you must focus only on the God within you and the God within all man. That is all that is required. You are not to make another man fearful if he does not worship in the way you see fit. Each man has his own journey home.

People have been killed for a different belief system at the hands of those who say they "believe." How distorted a thought that this would be correct and accepted by God. The ones who are judgmental and instill fear in others have set themselves up as god/guru and they should question themselves who they truly serve by doing this.

12

THE WINGED MONKEYS

"The obstacle is the path."
—Zen proverb

Off in the darkened castle, the wicked witch is busy sending her winged monkeys to collect Dorothy and her little dog. You can see by their countenance, they are eager to serve. Upon their leaving the castle, she tells them, "Don't worry, I've sent ahead a little insect to take the fight out of them."

In Baum's original version, she sends bees to sting them allowing the winged monkeys the ability to attack with little effort.

WIZDOM

How many times have you had the "fight" taken out

of you? Don't see it as something sent to beat you down; see the flip side of any challenge as something to strengthen your spirit.

Like the tempering of a sword, it is through the melt down, hammering, and cooling that the sword is made strong. It is the same with your soul and the challenges you meet in life. Each one is a gift—an opportunity created by you and by God to temper the soul.

Now, who are the winged monkeys? Has anyone questioned who these servants of the wicked witch might be?

Everything you have seen up to this point, is Dorothy's perception of her situation. She perceives the winged monkeys as evil because their intent is to take her to the castle of the wicked witch.

As in life, there are certain individuals who try your soul. You think of them as your enemy. But, as in the movies that you so like to watch, they only play a "role" in your personal drama. They are meant to be trying—at times, deviant, so that your soul, like an actor, can play off them. There will be times when you will play a supporting role in their life, thereby, assisting their life drama, as well.

If you look closely, you will see that the winged monkeys actually resemble gargoyles from the 11th century. As religious communities were trying to covert pagans to Christians, they turned pagan holidays into religious holy days and used images of gargoyles on top of their cathedrals as icons of protection. A question to ask; Why do you think

The Winged Monkeys

they are the chosen symbol sent to gather Dorothy and Toto? What do you think might be their purpose?

Their true mission is to take Dorothy where she fears to go—to the wicked witch's darkened castle; this representing the dark confines of Dorothy's own mind—the place where all her fears and negative thought patterns dwell. Dorothy is frightened as one would naturally be. What she doesn't know is that this is the very place she needs to go in order to deal with her fears and misconceptions of her life and herself.

The monkeys appear to everyone as evil. Surely, from their appearance, this seems true. But, knowing their history and how they are considered icons of protection, allows you to see them differently. This is the teaching: there will be times when you will be taken emotionally to frightening heights. Thoughts and events you perceive as bad, may not be; they, dear ones, may be the necessary event in your life that brings about enormous change for the better.

The winged entourage is now seen flying in the sky making a terrible noise; a terrifying scene that has scared countless children for years. Even as adults, it triggers many emotions to watch this scene. The sounds bring a chill to the body and reminds us of our fragility in the midst of a violent world.

The Wizdom of Oz

> *"As long as people use tactics*
> *to oppress or restrict other people*
> *from being free, there is work to be done."*
> —Rosa Parks

The monkeys are now upon the ground, rushing about, and our characters are divided. Dorothy and Toto are picked up and flown to a meeting with the unknown and possibly the unthinkable!

13

PICKING THEMSELVES UP

*"He'll lift you up and turn you around
and put your feet back on higher ground."*
—Van Morrison

In the aftermath of the rumble, there is panic and confusion. The scarecrow has been torn apart by the winged monkeys and left scattered on the ground while Dorothy and Toto have been whisked away to the witch's castle. Immediately, the tin man and lion go about the task of putting the scarecrow back together. They realize the need to unite in order to save Dorothy and Toto.

WIZDOM

It is by division that you are conquered. Symbolism

of the scarecrow being scattered about represents what can happen to you when caught in personal chaos; mental confusion and a scattering of your mind and personal energy. You could fall apart, so to speak.

Be centered within your being at the first sight or sign of chaos. Breathe deep—then deeper still. Hold that breath and let it out slowly. You must focus on the Divine Essence, God, that resides within you; you must ask for greater strength and spiritual protection.

It takes a lot of discipline not to fall into the mayhem that surrounds you. It's much easier to join the chaos than to ward it off, but will that serve you best? How do you feel physically and emotionally when you inadvertently allow yourself to be drawn in by those who wish to promote failure in your life by their negativity.

You must take a step back when one approaches with the pure poison of gossip or negative comments. Negativity is not only lethal to the mind, body and emotions but to the spirit as well.

When a global catastrophe occurs, you are immediately alarmed. Then the media that surrounds you takes you further in your fear by their multiple scenarios. Everyone is listening, believing and alarmed, and that leads to hopelessness and depression.

We do not wish to pick on the media for there are some fine journalists. It is the way it is presented to the people that is, at times, objectionable. The many people who watch in fear unknowingly create what is called a "mass consciousness of fear" that can affect others. As a space of global fear is created, man will feel overwhelmed by the chaos of thought and begin to believe that all good is lost.

You live in what is called "collective consciousness." This can be good or bad. The positive thoughts of others can create positive results. Likewise, negative thoughts produce negative results. When a group of people believe strongly in a certain idea or outcome; it can have an ocean wave effect on the people around them.

It is so very necessary for each individual to exercise the power of positive thought. Done on an individual basis by many, this can bring about a positive outcome in your immediate environment and, in turn, will bring about a favorable outcome for mankind.

If you are one who can get caught in the mayhem, why not be the one to see a positive outcome; the multi-possibility for a better world—a more peaceful world—your heaven here on Earth.

"IMAGINE"
—John Lennon

You are what you think. You are what you believe. Meditate upon this– ponder deeply how life might change if the people of the Earth refrained from getting involved in a negative outlook on life.

The Wizdom of Oz

Turn your vision away from the ugliness outside. Turn to your "inner vision" and create a beautiful outlook for tomorrow.

14

THE LONG AWAITED MEETING

*"I have a little shadow that goes in and out
with me and what can be
the use of him is more than I can see."*
—Robert Louis Stevenson

Upon her meeting with Dorothy, the witch says, "It's so nice of you to visit me in my loneliness."

Dorothy is terrified to be face to face with this dark being. Who is she? Why does she want these red slippers so desperately that she's willing to harm her and those who try to help?

Dorothy is unaware that the wicked witch is a fragmented piece of herself—the shadow side, the tormented side that you all may recognize. You know this entity—the judge and jury of your mind.

WIZDOM

It is now time for not only Dorothy to face the darker side of herself but a time for all of you to look also. You must not be afraid.

The witch feels it is nice that Dorothy has come at a time of loneliness. This is where man can be tripped up. When man is idle he may give in to his illusions of being "less-than"—a time when the recriminations come.

Remember, it can be very difficult to maintain a positive vision of oneself at all times; you may fall into judging, yourself and your life, harshly. If your tendency to berate yourself has become a habit, the following is something you can practice.

Because your world operates on polarity—North and South Pole, negative and positive, yin and yang, it will be necessary to learn the following: for all negative thoughts you might impose upon yourself, it is most necessary to follow with good ones. This one small act will keep your spirit up and moving in a positive direction with balance. Discipline and practice will be needed but this is how you will win the battles with yourself.

Remember that you are human and you are going to make mistakes. This is how you learn. You must allow yourself the space to make mistakes and forgive yourself and you must allow this for others.

If you look at your reflection, what you will see

The Long Awaited Meeting

mirrored back is only a small perception of your true self. The question to ponder is; "What is the inner image?" Careful—remember—not all of these perceptions belong to you. They are the "collective perceptions" that have been imposed upon your spirit by others. Whether they are good or bad—you have created only a small percentage.

Now, gently, if you strip away these perceptions and take another look, you can only find a beautiful spirit—shining bright—unencumbered; shining within and without! Now, take a deep breath and imprint this image upon your spirit's memory; you are now ready to move forward with your personal power and strength intact.

The witch covets the ruby slippers because they represent power to her—another's power. Her desire is so strong that she threatens to drown Toto if they are not given to her. Caring so much for her little dog, Dorothy is willing to relinquish them.

As the witch eagerly reaches to take them from Dorothy's feet, she is repelled by an electrical shock created by Dorothy's energy. The witch realizes that the slippers will elude her as long as Dorothy is alive and stands in her own power.

WIZDOM

The shadow side of your personality can never take you over as long as you stand in your truth. The truth is that you are a child of the Creator and you are loved unconditionally. A human cannot be taken down by darker thoughts and stand in this truth at the same time.

If you feel yourself falling under the spell of negative beliefs about yourself, visualize thoughts of your "Beginning"—your being created in the image and likeness of God.

In the next moment, while the witch muses on how to eliminate Dorothy, Toto escapes and rushes for the door. Dorothy cheers him on, "Run Toto, run"! He gets away.

The witch grows quite weary of Dorothy. She can't wait forever to get the slippers! She pulls out an hourglass to inform Dorothy that this will be the measure of time that she has left to live.

> *"You lock the door and throw away the key,*
> *There's someone in my head but it's not me"*
> —Pink Floyd

WIZDOM

Who or what is locked inside your head? What are the thoughts that drive you?

They are your memories—thought forms of your triumphs and failures. If you look closely, you will see them linked in their service to you. It is important that you not see your failures as something bad and wished to be hidden. Neither should you wallow in your triumphs. Both represent the blueprint of your soul's desire. As you grow in your learning, you will come to understand that some of your failures have actually promoted your triumphs!

You must get out of the habit of judging yourself in increments of good and bad. Be kinder to yourself and know that you are NOT a person with faults and failures but merely a traveler in search of self. If this is carried out, nothing can be a mistake or failure because it supports your journey on Earth; allow yourself to fully appreciate all aspects of your personhood and give gratitude for the miracle called life.

There is a reward of seeing your life this way. As you accept yourself, there will be less judgment; cultivating forgiveness and love within you. In addition, by this personal cultivation, you will lessen your judgments of others, creating an environment of unconditional love.

You can see how the energies of the heavens could be created in the here and now by just this one act.

The Wizdom of Oz

> *"Love has no other desire*
> *but to fulfill itself"*
> —Kahil Gibran

Dorothy is terribly frightened by the threat of extinction. She weeps as she watches the sand run through the hourglass. In her despair, she hears her Auntie Em calling out to her, "Dorothy, Dorothy."

Dorothy follows the voice to a vision of her dear Auntie Em in the witch's crystal ball! Through her tears, Dorothy recounts everything that has happened since she left, crying, "I'm frightened Auntie Em, I'm frightened"—she feels her time is running out.

> *"Hanging in quiet desperation is the English way,*
> *the time is gone, the song is over,*
> *Thought I'd have something more to say."*
> —Pink Floyd

WIZDOM

On a subconscious level, you seem to understand that your time is limited. You also have felt that the sands of time are working against you—a feeling of time running out.

The Long Awaited Meeting

Dismiss that thought and surrender yourself to the pleasure of being in the present moment.

There is no beginning and no end. All moments are to be seen as one connected to another; like nature with its seasons, you are the continuous pure extension of God, recreating yourself time and time again.

Look once again at the Earth. With attention and a deep awareness, pay attention to the coming and going of the seasons. Does this speak to your heart as an ending or a cycle?

You have many symbols around you that speak of these cycles; the waxing and waning of the moon; the rise and descent of the sun. Nature provides the mysteries and the answers. Why do you feel that you would be extinguished should you not take another breath? Are you not as important as the rest of creation? Do you not fully understand that you hold the essence of the universe—God—within your very being?

Your light and essence continues to flourish after your physical death and is returned to the Source—God—All That Is.

Time will never run out for you— for you are timeless.

Auntie Em's image fades from the crystal ball replaced by the wicked witch who mimics Dorothy's child-like but very real fear!

WIZDOM

Look out! When you least expect it, your darker side will mock you and try to take you down. It will not just try this but will tempt, terrorize and shake you to the core of your being if needed.

Some will want to run away from this encounter. Some will indulge themselves in addictions in order not to confront. You may at times think you have gotten away by avoidance—not so. When the time is right, you will have this confrontation and, we say, why put this off when it means the exaltation of your spirit?

What a drama! Or is it? What fuels this part of you that possesses so much power—enough to bring you to a point of hopelessness and despair?

The answer is quite simple—the application challenging. You must not give in to the inner dialogue that tells you constantly that you are imperfect. You must do your best to show no fear and express, out loud if necessary, that "all is well" in spite of how your situation in life may appear. By this small but powerful gesture, you will show the confidence of a spiritual being and darkness cannot exist in the environment of a fearless spirit!

15

TO THE RESCUE

*"It's not the size of the dog in the fight,
it's the size of the fight in the dog."*
—Anonymous

Toto returns to Dorothy's friends in the forest where he urges them to follow him to the castle to rescue her before it's too late. Unaware, Tin Man, Scarecrow, and Lion start to show signs of the very things they seek: the tin man starts to cry—displaying a heart; the scarecrow says, he will *think* of a plan demonstrating his ability to form thoughts; and the lion bravely says he will lead—with some persuasion from the others!

Through this crisis, they become unified in their efforts, tapping into their inner abilities and develop inner strength.

WIZDOM

There are some who might think that a crisis is God's punishment. Some might just feel it is a stroke of bad luck and some may be enlightened to see crisis as the opportunity it is.

Man has shown time and time again what he can do under pressure. His inner spirit knows it only as a test and rises to the challenge. He may at times feel put upon and stretched to his very limit but he will still find that extra measure of strength to follow through.

This doesn't happen with everyone. Some do fall under the pressure and are seemingly wiped out. When this takes place, we cannot view this as a failure but have an understanding that there is more inner work to be done.

You are asked to do your best with such crisis. See the potential it holds—a chance to grow strong in your faith—an opportunity to learn forgiveness and compassion. Ask your heavenly Father for extra help and guidance during trying times so that you might remain strong and unified in your spirit.

Nothing works against you. It may feel that way at times, but everything is part of the Divine Plan. Look for the lessons these situations may bring. Give gratitude for the gift of awareness that follows.

To the Rescue

"OOO – EE – HO"

Unbeknownst to our threesome, the soldiers of the witch, called Winkies, have discovered them. A fight ensues, leaving them to their own defense.

> *"Us and them and after all, we're only ordinary men—me and you"*
> —Pink Floyd

The next scene shows them victorious, dressed in the soldiers' clothing and making their way into the castle. Should you look closely at the soldiers, you see another piece of the illusion—they are the same; dressed alike and marching in formation, representing the "programmed thinking" that has gained power over Dorothy up to this moment. Our threesome, by their diversity, represent the introduction of new thoughts that have an ability to bring about change and affect outcomes. In Dorothy's case, it is only a matter of time before that happens!

WIZDOM

Diversity forces mankind to think and question.

As they enter the castle, they branch off to find Dorothy with Toto leading the way.

You may have noticed, at this point, that I have not touched on the personality of this brave little dog who has fastened himself to Dorothy and her journey. There has been a reason. To have addressed his presence early on, you would not have seen his full potential. Thinking back on all the situations in which Dorothy has found herself, you will note that Toto was always by her side and was always the catalyst for change. Let's flash back—

Getting into the Alvira Gulch's garden begins Dorothy's flight
Is taken from Dorothy by order of the sheriff
Escapes and returns to Dorothy
Is caught up in tornado with Dorothy
Is threatened by the wicked witch; "I'll get you my pretty and your little dog, too!"
Stays by her side throughout
Is captured by witch
Escapes—runs for help
Leads others to Dorothy
(with more events to follow!)

WIZDOM

Who is this magical creature that is a constant figure

in this drama? Could he also be like the angel, Glinda? Through his unique actions, he provides comfort, guidance, protection and unconditional love—all angelic qualities.

Look at the animals of the Earth. See their connection to the world as well as the human race. Look at the animals that you have chosen or who have chosen you. Who are they? What energy do they carry and why have they chosen to journey with you at this time?

Animals who have chosen to live directly with humans have an interconnectedness to them. They are angels in disguise.

*In Loving Memory And Gratitude;
Our family dog of 14 years, "Roxanne"*

16

ASHES, ASHES—
WE ALL FALL DOWN

*"The Infinite Mind of THE ALL
is the womb of Universes."*
—The Kybalion

As they find Dorothy and start to make their escape, the witch and her followers find and corner them. They try to run a different way but are blocked once again! The witch decides it's time to get rid of them one by one. She begins by setting fire to the scarecrow, for he is a powerful ally to Dorothy, representing her logic. The witch chants, "Ring around the rosy" – that line finished is; "a pocket full of posies. Ashes, ashes, we all fall down."

WIZDOM

As the consciousness of individuals can raise the consciousness of the planet, by the same token, you can also "all fall down." Even though there appears to be separation among people, the truth is that you belong to and inspire one another. This is an energetic truth; you are a speck of Creation—the Universe—God. The lessons among you cannot be separated because each person's actions and reactions affect the next.

This an important lesson for your planet. Until you come to the realization that "all is One" there will continue to be strife among you and within you.

Think for a moment. Why has diversity been a component of life on Earth? Is it only to irritate and divide those among you? Would that appear to be a grand plan?

Diversity is on your planet to promote knowledge, understanding and acceptance. Diversity offers man an opportunity to grow in compassion and love. How can one claim to be a "believer" and hold hate in his heart for another being? It is impossible.

Bless the differences among you. See the diversity of people as a gift— one sent to assist you in emulating the One through whom "all" things have been created.

Nothing and no one is to be hated or destroyed. Only through unification will you be raised.

Now, that's a grand plan!

Dorothy is horrified when the witch sets the scarecrow on fire. He has not only been her friend but represents her own logic. She is not willing to let either of them go.

Once again, Dorothy stands up against adverse conditions, all the while developing and flexing her spiritual muscles. She defies the witch's actions by throwing water on the scarecrow. In one crazy moment, the water misses the mark and hits the witch who becomes hysterical! Unknown to the others, it is the element of water that ultimately destroys the wicked witch by melting her into a puddle of nothingness!

"I'm melting away, what a world, what a world. Who would have thought a good little girl like you could have destroyed my beautiful wickedness."
—The Wicked Witch

WIZDOM

The element of water was not the only instrument

that destroyed the wicked witch and her terrible manners. Think of her last words; they are very powerful—"Who would have thought a good little girl like you could have destroyed my beautiful wickedness?"

The wicked witch did not see Dorothy as strong. She saw her only as a small defenseless child. She carelessly misjudged and did not consider the power of "innocence" in the child before her. Yet, she found it to be her destroyer.

Become like the child who rides the carousel with joy and no expectations. Become a responsible parent to the child that lives within you.

Some guidelines: know that you are now the caretaker of this child. Don't push him/her so hard and fast; don't demand perfection. Take care of your inner child's physical needs, making sure enough exercise, sleep and nutrition is available. Incorporate prayer and meditation and if the proverbial bully shows up in the form of fear trying to terrorize your child; SHOW FEAR THE DOOR—IMMEDIATELY!!

Remember, fear cannot stay alive when facing the optimism and pure faith of a child. When you come to understand that all aspects of your life are a part of God's plan, you will then come to understand that all things that befall you are in your best interest only; that your spirit has taken on the Earth mission willingly; that the one you call God has gifted you with every asset to go about this business of growth. By developing this awareness, the fears, bullies and inner demons will cease to exist. They will simply melt away.

Dorothy fears what the soldiers will do to them now. She tries to explain that she really didn't mean to kill the wicked witch; she only wanted to put the fire out. Much to everyone's surprise, the Winkies are very grateful for their liberation—they cheer, "Hail to Dorothy!"

> *"As we are liberated from our own fear,
> our presence automatically liberates others"*
> —Marriane Williamson

WIZDOM

What a wonderful word—liberation. From what do you wish to be liberated? Fear? Anxiety?

Questions to ponder: Could it be man's early programmed thinking that brings so much anxiety to the planet? Is that where man's fears and misconceptions lie? At this time in history, certain thought patterns will need to be destroyed in order to allow mankind more joy in this beautiful garden called Earth.

You will be called upon, one by one, to question any fear-based perception in your life. You will be asked to go to the core, likened to the core of your Earth, to tap into the fire of your inner wisdom. You will then begin to enjoy the freedom of making good choices by pausing and asking yourself if a person or situation "feels right" to you.

Do not be like the soldiers who served the wicked witch by giving homage to the fears she created. Be brave. Dare to be different! Your dream is your dream! In the practice of this, you will allow others to follow theirs.

17

SEEKING VALIDATION

"The time for the healing of the wounds has come. The moment to bridge the chasms that divide us has come."
—Nelson Mandela

After much travail, our wayward travelers proudly return to the wizard with the witch's broom in hand. They still hope that he will give them the gifts they have requested, not understanding that they have already developed the qualities they desired.

The wizard is surprised at their return; he has not counted on this. He tells them to go away and return tomorrow but they protest loudly as the wizard tries to drown their voices out by his own.

It is time for the illusion to be unveiled and Toto, once again, is a key player. Gingerly, he walks towards the curtain, pulls it back and exposes the wizard in his pretense.

> *"Pay no attention to the man
> behind the curtain."*

They are shocked, disappointed and angered to find out the wizard is only a mere mortal, the doorman, who has tricked them. All their hopes and wishes evaporate as Dorothy scolds him, "You're a very bad man." The wizard protests her cry of disappointment. He explains, he is not really a bad man—just a very bad wizard.

> *"I keep my ideals,
> because in spite of everything,
> I still believe that people are really good at heart."*
> —Anne Frank

WIZDOM

In your personal cinema, you will NOT find your God as false. What you may discover is that your perception of Him may be somewhat distorted.

At times, you have seen your God as the giver of things with the power to punish and take it all away should you appear unworthy. You must realize that your mere existence deems you worthy.

If you feel corrupted, it has been derived from man—God's power is unconditional love. Part of your mission is to understand this truth. In coming to understand this, you will not only have an ability to love yourself but others as well. Only then can you experience Heaven on Earth—only then.

> *"If you don't get it from yourself,*
> *where will you go for it?"*
> —Buddhist Saying

The gentleman behind the curtain decides to exercise his personal wizardry by giving them items that will acknowledge their personal growth—the outward sign of validation they have so desired.

To the scarecrow, he presents a diploma. The new self-empowered wizard states that he can give this to him, as he was an elected member of a committee from the University of E Pluribus Unum—"out of the many, one."

> *"I think, therefore, I am."*
> —Rene Descartes

Turning his attention to the lion, the wizard says, "My friend, you are a victim of disorganized thinking.

Seeking Validation

You have confused courage with wisdom." He gives him a medal of honor—a Triple Cross for bravery against wicked witches—and makes him a member of The Legion of Courage.

> *"God grant me the serenity*
> *To accept the things I cannot change,*
> *The courage to*
> *change the things I can,*
> *And the wisdom to know the difference."*
> —Dr. Reinhold Niebuhr

To the tin man, he gives a heart shaped ticking clock; the gift coming with guidance; "A heart is not judged by how much you love but how much you are loved by others."

> *"Oz never gave nothing to the tin man that he didn't, didn't already have."*
> —America

WIZDOM

What makes you feel whole and content? What outward sign do you require in order to feel successful? Could it be the home you've been planning? Is it the car with all the buttons? Is it lots of money?

All of the aforementioned items are certainly nice things to acquire and may indicate to others and to yourself that you are indeed a success in the material sense. But, it is known, that people can have all of these things and still feel empty.

Ponder what truly rewards a person on his/her journey. Some questions to ask yourself are the following: Do you have the capacity to love unconditionally? Do others love you? Have you been able to influence and give hope to another? Will you leave this planet, not as you found it, but better?

You do not need an outward sign to feel complete. What you hold within is important to your spirit and will gauge your success as well as your happiness.

Do not wait on another to validate your spirit, for it may never come. Rely only on yourself and the God within you for validation.

In the midst of their excitement, they realize that Dorothy has been left out—"What about Dorothy?"

What Dorothy needs cannot be easily given; she is deeply saddened by this thought. However, much to her surprise, the professor offers to take her home, himself, in a hot-air balloon that he stored upon his arrival at Emerald City. He says, "My dear Dorothy, you and I will return to the land of E Pluribus Unum"—out of the many, one!

WIZDOM

Dorothy so desires to get back to her original state—Kansas. There is a burning desire within each of you to return to your "original state"—the state of grace, beauty, and oneness.

> *"So the child grew and became strong in spirit."*
> —Luke 1:80

18

YOU HAVE ALWAYS HAD THE POWER

*"You're packing a suitcase for a place
none of us has been—
a place that has to be believed to be seen."*
—Bono (of U2)

Dorothy, Toto and the professor prepare to leave. Standing in the basket of the multi-colored hot air balloon, the professor bids farewell to the people of Emerald City. Then, without warning, Toto spies a cat and jumps from Dorothy arms. Running after Toto, she calls out to the professor to wait.

In the meantime, the ropes from the balloon loosen and the professor leaves without her. All appears lost for poor Dorothy. Extremely saddened, she says, "I'll never get home." The tin man, scarecrow and lion proclaim their love for Dorothy telling her, "Stay with us Dorothy. We all love you; we don't want you to go." Dorothy replies, "That is very kind of you but this could never be like Kansas."

WIZDOM

This lovely child still carries with her the memory of her home—her state of bliss. She cannot feel content while feeling separated from the One she loves most—her Creator.

Humans have a tendency to hold on to their loved ones at the hour of their spirit passing from this world to the next—to the Source of their beginning. They, too, say, "We love you and will miss you," and this is true.

But, we would like to go further by saying the true reason for man's tears runs deeper than you know; he experiences a feeling a being left behind—a feeling of celestial separation.

Through each physical death, you are taught the value of living. You are asked also to see the value of death— the physical death—the process of "returning home."

When you are faced with the death of a loved one, you must be kind to their soul and give them permission to leave. Allow them to know that you will be fine until your next meeting with them.

Remember, it is only a thin veil that will separate you. Give them your prayers and good wishes, release them and let them go peacefully. This can take place at their actual transition time and days beyond.

Assist them in their leaving as you did in their living.

A ball of light suddenly appears and the scarecrow says, "Look, here is someone who can help you." Glinda arrives, once again, and Dorothy asks, "Will you help me? Can you help me?"

In all her splendor Glinda replies, "You don't need to be helped any longer,

You've always had the power.

Her friends ask, "Why didn't you tell her before?" Glinda replies, "She wouldn't have believed me—she had to learn it for herself."

WIZDOM

Are not all lessons cherished when they come from discovery? Think of your own personal discoveries—the excitement in the find.

The Earth and its people are progressing at a fast pace, spiritually. They will come to understand and accept their personal power.

You Have Always Had the Power

How wonderful to lose the signature of sinner and rejoice in the knowledge of your power and holiness! How liberating to come to the understanding that all things come from Oneness and return to Oneness.

You may think that you are very small and plain upon your planet, but we say you are the Wizard and Oz resides in you!

Dorothy's friends ask, "What have you learned Dorothy?" She replies, "If I ever go looking for my heart's desire again, I won't look any further than my own back yard because, if it isn't there, I never really lost it to begin with."

WIZDOM

What have you learned? That will be the question upon leaving this planet. Did you learn compassion, forgiveness and unconditional love? Did you receive your heart and use your brain? Were you courageous in your endeavors—did you develop faith in a Higher Order? Will you be happy with the way you leave things in this World or will some things be left undone?

You must strive to do the very best with the gifts you

have been given. Nothing more is asked of you. In the end, you will judge your life and you will have to find peace with it.

> *Show yourself compassion—Now*
> *Encourage yourself—Now*
> *Celebrate your personal victories—Now*
> *Rise up from your perceived failures—Now*
> *Find peace, Now!*

At some point in your existence, you will be summoned to return to the Source from whence you came. It will be the soul's desire to tell of this journey in a foreign land—how you went about looking here and there for peace and happiness only to find out that it was within you all the time.

The heavens will rejoice upon your return and revel in your stories!

> "And ye shall know the truth
> and the truth shall set you free."
> —Jesus, John 8:31

As Dorothy prepares to leave, she sadly realizes it

is time for her to say goodbye to her fellow travelers, her friends, who have served her so well. This act will bring about the conclusion of Dorothy's journey and is symbolic of her spiritual evolution.

WIZDOM

In kissing the lion goodbye—she releases all her fears; In kissing the tin man, she releases her emotional attachments to outcomes; In kissing the scarecrow, she says, "I think I will miss you the most; she is now ready to release her logic/ego and is now ready to go home—to the innermost part of her being where only true peace resides.

This is Dorothy's physical leaving of the Earth and returning home; back to Oneness. You see, Dorothy's lesson was to understand that home exists "here" as well as "there." Now, she can embrace this feeling no matter where she is for she has found "home" within herself; her mission accomplished!

Glinda poses the question to Dorothy: "Are you ready now?" Dorothy takes one more look around her and says, "Yes, I'm ready."

WIZDOM

Are you ready now? Are you ready to make a commitment to the journey of self-learning— to take responsibility for your life.

Don't worry about what another is doing, for it will not benefit you to do so. Each person's walk is different and so are his perceptions. Keep to your path and don't delay. Your future lies in this moment!

Dorothy then clicks her heels and says, "There's no place like home, there's no place like home."

> *"Take my hand, love,*
> *I'm taking you home."*
> —Don Henley

You Have Always Had the Power

TAKE A MOMENT AND FEEL YOUR CONNECTION
YOU ARE NOT SEPARATE—YOU ARE ONE

Allow yourself to feel –
(Breathe)
Feel your connection to the Earth -
(Breathe)
Feel your connection to the heavens -
(Breathe)

(breathe & affirm to yourself)

"balance in all things"
"balance in all things"
"balance in all things"
Now, breathe –

"There's no place like home"
There's no place like home"
"There's no place like home"

I am in the present moment –
I am home

19

BACK TO HER ORIGINAL STATE

> *"So long ago*
> *Was it in a dream,*
> *was it just a dream?*
> *I know, yes I know*
> *Seemed so very real,*
> *it seemed so real to me."*
> —John Lennon

Dorothy finds herself back home, in her own bed, surrounded by family and friends. She tries to tell them where she has been and what has happened. "I tried to get back for days and days" –symbolic of many lifetimes– "and you were there, and you were there..." –symbolic of our reuniting with loved ones after physical death.

Her family and friends chuckle at her delusion. She

is told that during the storm her head was injured; what she had experienced was only a dream.

Yet, Dorothy emphatically states, "It wasn't a dream, it was a place! This was a truly live place and I remember that some of it wasn't very nice but most of it was beautiful, but just the same, all I kept saying to everyone was I want to go home and they sent me home."

WIZDOM

The world, as you know it, is your waking dream, at times mere illusion.

Is the life you experience in all manners your true reality, or just one made up by others? Within the soul lies a desire to experience and walk upon the Earth in order to come to a better understanding of creation as an expression of the Creator.

The soul at times lives in a vacuum, a void of sorts, and contemplates its part in the universe. It is on the Earth plane that the soul can experience, with the cooperation of the human body, mind and heart—its reality.

The sad drama of coming to the Earth is; as you take on a human body, you lose the memory of your spirit and risk getting caught in the web of the illusions of others. As you grow older, you begin to exist and forget to experience. It then becomes important to be the smartest, most beautiful and acquire great wealth—all prisoners of the thoughts of others.

Everyone is susceptible to fall under this spell and when they do, cease to be happy. The way out is to be whoever you came here to be! This is your life, your expression and experience!

Should you not like your present reality, create a new one; one with appreciation and love for the beautiful creation that you ARE!

Look to the children and become more like them. Their creative expression is happiness in a most simple manner. They do not know whether they are physically beautiful, smart, or wealthy. They have the quality to be happy with the smallest of things. They do not understand religion or politics. They are not prejudiced. A baby does not cry because someone next to him is not the correct race, creed, or color. Woe to the man who teaches hatred to the little ones for that same hatred will be returned to him and cause destruction of his spirit. Children come to teach and are taught. Watch them closely and become more like them. Let them show you the way.

Back to Her Original State

"Verily, I say unto you, whosoever shall not receive the kingdom of God as a little child he shall not enter therein."
—Mark 10:15

"But anyway, Toto, we're home. I'm not going to leave here ever, ever again."

"Oh Auntie Em"
(* "Me" spelled backwards*)

"THERE'S NO PLACE LIKE HOME"

A MESSAGE FROM THE AUTHOR

Our journey begins with one step on the path of illumination. The journey is within. We must cultivate the gifts given to us by our Creator and we must never, for one moment, feel alone.

The gift of intelligence brought us to the Earth. It is the heart we ponder and it is with courage, we will not fail. Recognize all these gifts as one—not to be separated.

We also need to bless the shadow side of ourselves—our negative perceptions, our thoughts of failure and our emotional pain. For they serve us as inspiration to search for our inner beauty and truth.

Seek not the wizard, the One who created us in His likeness, for He lives within us. Let our eyes see the Earth and its inhabitants as He sees them. Let our words be His words. Let our hearts that beat in rhythm with the Earth, be His also.

And, so it is, that each person we encounter is on the same journey of seeking and expression as ourselves. Enlightenment and awareness of this are keys to the city.

In addition, should we become tired on our journey–

STOP – only momentarily
BREATHE – to expand our light within and
REMEMBER – who we are in the truest and highest sense
Then, my friends, continue—

SOME THOUGHTS FOR YOUR JOURNEY

- You are not just living life; you are life
- You can't move forward as long as you are looking back
- Be patient with yourself
- Read inspirational material
- Take a news fast
- Keep a gratitude journal
- Make life a little easier for others daily
- Regard your body—appreciate its abilities and don't linger on disabilities
- Old saying: "Don't do anything to anyone that you would not like done to you"
- New saying: Don't create bad karma
- A dog has four legs, but can only move in one direction
- Don't judge your life in increments of good and bad; enjoy the entire journey
- It is an old saying, "What doesn't kill you makes you strong"
- This too shall pass
- Forgive others as you would like to be forgiven
- Smile or laugh at least once a day
- Guide and protect the children of the Earth; Enlighten, Encourage, and Love
- You are a spiritual being having a human experience
- Don't watch violence—movies or television; It is damaging to the soul

- Don't measure your life against others
- Cultivate your creativity
- Live in the present moment
- Be watchful of your thoughts today for they create your tomorrow
- Journal
- Walk in nature
- Be kind to animals
- Meditate
- Communicate
- Consummate
- Be joyful. Keep the light you were given at birth glowing and return brighter than you left

Have a wonderful journey!

*"I finally found my peace of mind,
beyond the yellow brick road…"*
—Sir Elton John

ACKNOWLEDGEMENTS

We gratefully acknowledge the following sources.

—Page 1. Feltenstein, George; *The Wizard of Oz*. Produced by Jesse Kaye. Turner Entertainment & Turner Broadcasting System, Inc, 1939, 1956.

—Page 2. Feltenstein, George; *The Wizard of Oz*. Produced by Jesse Kaye. Turner Entertainment & Turner Broadcasting System, Inc, 1939, 1956.

—page 4. *The Holy Bible*. Romans 8:31.

—page 5. *The Holy Bible*. John 14:27.

—page 6. Inscription on Temple of Apollo at Delphi; Plato, *Protagorus*, 343 B.C.

—page 7. Dylan, Bob. Subterranean Homesick Blues; *Bootleg Series (rare & unreleased)* 1961 – 1991 Sony Entertainment, Inc (p) Sony Music Entertainment, 1991.

—page 11. Wilde, Oscar. *The Decay of Lying* in *Intentions*, London, Methuen & Co., 1891.

—page 14. Barrie, J.M. *Peter Pan*. Henry Holt & Co., Inc., 2003.

—page 17. Pink Floyd. *The Dark Side of the Moon*. EMI Records, LTD. 1973. Manufactured by Capital Records, Inc., 2003.

—page 19. Dickinson, Emily. *The Complete Book of Poems of Emily Dickinson*. Boston; Little, Brown & Company Publisher, 1924.

—page 20. Baum, L. Frank; *The Wonderful Wizard of Oz.* 1900.

—page 21. McCartney, Paul. Let it Be Soundtrack. Capitol Records, 1970.

—page 21. Feltenstein, George; *The Wizard of Oz.* Produced by Jesse Kaye. Turner Entertainment & Turner Broadcasting System, Inc, 1939, 1956.

—page 22. Shinn, Florence. *The Game of Life and How To Play It;* © 1925 DeVorss & Company, Publisher.

—page 26. Moulthrop, Glenna Hammer. *Living in Love; A Compilation of Mother Teresa's Teachings on Love.* TowleHouse Publishing Co., Inc., 2000.

—page 31. *The Holy Bible.* John 15:13.

—page 33. Shakespeare, William. *As You Like It.*

—page 34. *The Holy Bible.* Psalms, 23rd verse.

—page 38. *The Wizard of Oz* © Loew's Incorporated. MGM UA Home Video, Inc. and Turner Entertainment Co, 1991.

—page 44. Winfrey, Oprah. *O Magazine*, August 2001

—page 45. *The Wizard of Oz* © Loew's Incorporated. MGM UA Home Video, Inc. and Turner Entertainment Co., 1991.

—page 46. *The Holy Bible.* Mathew 7:7.

—page 47. Simon, Carly. *Greatest Hits Live,* Produced by Carly Simon and Tom "T-Bone" Wolk, Arista Records, Inc., 1988.

—page 51. *The Holy Bible.* Mathew 6:10.

—page 55. Dumas, A. *The Three Musketeers*. Random House Trade Paperbacks, 1981.

—page 59. Tom Hanks, New Year's Philosophy, *Tonight Show*, January 2000

—page 60. U2, "Beautiful Day"; *All That You Can't Leave Behind*, Universal International Music, BV, 2000.

—page 66. Parks, Rosa. *Quiet Strength;* Rosa Parks with Gregory J. Reed, Zondervan Publishing House, 1994.

—page 67. Morrison, Van. *Avalon Sunset*, Caledonia Productions, LTD; Manufactured by A&M Records, 1989.

—page 69. Lennon, John. *Imagine.* Capitol Records, 2000.

—page 71. Stevenson, Robert Louis, *A Child's Garden of Verses*. First Publishing 1885; Delecorte Press/New York.

—page 74. Pink Floyd. *The Dark Side of the Moon*. EMI Records, LTD. 1973. Manufactured by Capital Records, Inc., 2003.

—page 76. Gibran, Kahil. *The Prophet.* Administrators C.T.A. of Kahil Gibran Estate & Mary G. Gibran, 1923, 1951.

—page 76. Pink Floyd. *The Dark Side of the Moon*. EMI Records, LTD. 1973. Manufactured by Capital Records, Inc., 2003.

—page 81. Pink Floyd. *The Dark Side of the Moon*. EMI Records, LTD. 1973. Manufactured by Capital Records, Inc., 2003.

—page 84. The Kybalion; A *Study of the Hermetic*

Philosophy of Ancient Egypt and Greece; by Three Initiates; © 1908,1936 The Yogi Publication Society; Republished 1988, Tri-State Press, Clayton, Georgia.

—page 86. *The Wizard of Oz* © Loew's Incorporated. MGM UA Home Video, Inc. and Turner Entertainment Co., 1991.

—page 88. Williamson, Marriane. *A Return to Love: Reflections on the Principles of A Course in Miracles.* Perennial, 1993, Harper Collins, Publishers, Inc.

—page 90. Nelson Mandela, Inaugural speech delivered Pretoria, May 10, 1994.

—page 91. Frank, Anne. *Diary of a Young Girl.* A Bantam Book/by arrangement with Doubleday. Doubleday Publishing; 1967/Bantam edition,1993.

—page 93. America, *Greatest Hits History,* Warner Bros. Records, A Time Warner Company © & (P) Turner Broadcasting System, Inc. © Warner Bros. Records, Inc., 1975.

—page 95. *The Holy Bible.* Luke 1:80

—page 96. U2, "Beautiful Day"; *All That You Can't Leave Behind*, Universal International Music, BV, 2000.

—page 100. *The Holy Bible.* John 8:31.

—page 102. Henley, Don. *Inside Job;* Produced by Don Henley & Stan Lynch/ Warner Bros. Records, © Warner Bros. Records, Inc., 2000.

—page 104. Lennon, John. *Number Nine Dream.* Lennon Legend, *The Very Best of John Lennon*, (p) 1997 -

compilation is owned by EMJ Records, LTD; © 1997 EMI Record, LTD.

—page 107. *The Holy Bible.* Mark 10:15.

—page 111. John, Elton. *One Night Only, The Greatest Hits*; © 1973 Island Records.

www.ingramcontent.com/pod-product-compliance
Lightning Source LLC
Chambersburg PA
CBHW020910090426
42736CB00008B/562